HOW 2 B HAPPY :-)

Get the happy habit!

J. Alexander

We would like to thank Rosie Alexander, Chris Alton,
Helen Clutterbuck, Calum Gilligan, Louisa Goodfellow, Liz Kessler
and Joseph Knight for their help in reviewing this book

First published in 2006 by
A & C Black Publishers Ltd
38 Soho Square, London, W1D 3HB

www.acblack.com

Designed by Giraffic Design
Edited by Mary-Jane Wilkins

ISBN 0-7136-7559-4
ISBN 978-0-7136-7559-7

A CIP catalogue for this book is available from the British Library

A & C Black uses paper produced with elemental chlorine-free pulp,
harvested from managed, sustainable forests.

Printed and bound in Great Britain by Bookmarque Ltd, Croydon, Surrey

Contents

First the facts

The present is a gift! It's a pun – present, gift? But seriously, it is. You didn't ask for life, you didn't work and save up for it – yet here it is, bursting with people, places and experiences.

What kind of gift is it for you? Is it like the amazing all-singing, all-dancing sound system at the top of your Christmas list? Or is it more like those sweaters your great auntie knits for you? (She means well but if you ever wore one outside the house you'd have to change your name and move to Greenland!)

The scale of 1 to wonderful

Find a piece of paper and draw a line like this one, with the numbers 1-10 on it. Now decide how the important things in your life score on the scale.

terrible		tolerable		a bit mixed
1	2	3	4	5

■ Think about your family – what's annoying about them? What's great? Mark an **F** on your scale to show how you rate them.

■ Think about school – what's annoying about it? What's great? Mark an **S** to show where school comes on your scale.

■ Think about your leisure time – what's boring? What's great? Mark an **L** for this.

■ Think about the future – is the outlook sunny or bleak and overcast? Mark an **O** on your scale for how you rate the outlook just now.

Add the scores together, divide by 4 and hey presto! You can see what kind of present you have.

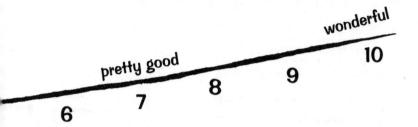

wonderful

pretty good

6 7 8 9 10

5

Results

If you scored...

The full 10 points *Amazing! Not many people are as happy with their life as you are.*

7, 8 or 9 points *Lucky you! You appreciate what you have.*

4, 5 or 6 points *Not surprising. Lots of people feel mildly fed up with some aspect of their life.*

3 points or less *Don't worry (you're stressed enough already!). You're actually quite normal...*

'I beg your pardon!' I hear you say. 'How can less than tolerable be normal?' Well in recent surveys, 50% of 10-year-olds and 90% of 14-year-olds said they often felt bogged down by sadness and anxiety. And it isn't just kids. Millions of older people get pills from their doctor to help them cope, or spend a fortune on therapy. So what's going on?

Well for starters we have some pretty weird ideas about happiness these days, and that's why I'm going to begin this book with five fascinating facts.

Five fascinating facts

1 Even happy people can't be happy all the time

In a perfect world, we could all be happy all the time, but this isn't a perfect world.

Suppose:

- *your hamster dies*
- *your best band splits up*
- *your mum won't buy you the trainers you want*
- *you do really badly in tests*

You're bound to feel fed up!

And what about all the things you want that you don't have, for example:

- *a billion pounds*
- *a brain like Einstein's*
- *your own TV show*
- *all the sweets you can eat*

It's enough to get anyone down!

Unhappy feelings aren't just inevitable – they have a purpose too.

They can spur you on to try harder

For example, suppose you do really badly in a maths test. You're going to feel fed up with yourself and that means you'll do more revision next time because you won't want to feel that way again.

They can inspire you to be stronger

For example, suppose you had the chance to meet your football hero, but you hung back because you were shy. You'd feel so cross with yourself that next time you'd get over your shyness because you wouldn't want to feel that way again.

They can keep you safe

For example, maybe you're out after dark when you shouldn't be and you feel scared – you'll remember how horrible that feels and make sure you get home earlier next time.

They can help you learn from your mistakes

Have you ever felt guilty about something?
Uncomfortable, isn't it? You wouldn't want to
do the same again!

Life's full of setbacks and frustrations and it's
natural to be down in the dumps sometimes, but
you don't have to stay there. Happy people get
knocked down too – they're just much quicker
at bouncing back.

2 Happiness has nothing to do with how much money you've got

Most people think they'd be happier if they had pots
of money, but research shows that the feel-good
effect of getting richer doesn't last. You soon grow
used to it, and however
rich you are there's still
something you can't afford.

Even people who
win millions of pounds
on the lottery go back
to their previous level
of happiness once the
excitement has worn off.

Happy fact :-)

Research shows that
wealth makes no
difference to how
happy people are
except at the extremes
of ridiculously rich or
extremely poor.

After the first spending spree, the grumpy ones go back to grumbling – only now they complain about their gardener/cleaner/personal shopper instead of their bus driver or boss. The cheerful ones still enjoy themselves – only now they go sailing in the Seychelles instead of camping in Cornwall.

Compared with our parents and grandparents, most of us are like lottery winners. Most of us have more money than people have ever had before, with all sorts of benefits, such as cars and TVs, mobile phones, central heating, computers, affordable clothes and fast foods, but we don't seem to be any happier at all.

So although a bit more pocket money wouldn't go amiss, it wouldn't make you happier in the long term either. **Strange but true!**

3 Happiness has nothing to do with looks or personality

Some people are happy even though they're as plain as porridge, and other people are unhappy even though they look like supermodels. So if you think being stick-thin and getting a great haircut is going to make you happy – well, maybe not. This is actually quite a cheerful thought for those of us who have a wobbly body and a stroppy hairdresser.

Here's another cheerful thought. You don't have to have a particular sort of personality. Most of us think of happy people as being outgoing, sporty and popular, but plenty of quiet types are blissfully happy doing their own thing.

4 Happiness doesn't depend on what happens to you

Bad things happen to everybody, but not everybody is ground down by them. I had a friend at school who fell off a motorbike and damaged her leg so badly that it ended up an inch shorter than the other one Did she let it get her down? No – she said she was just happy to be alive.

And then there's my gran. She lived through two world wars, brought up four children and could hardly pay the rent, but her motto was 'Mustn't grumble!'

Difficult events and circumstances may make it harder to be happy, but they don't have to make it impossible.

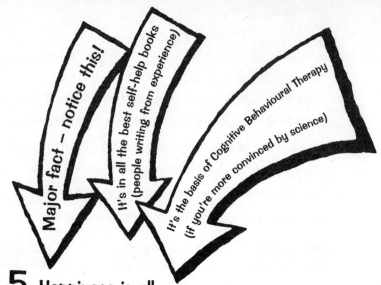

Major fact – notice this!

It's in all the best self-help books (people writing from experience)

It's the basis of Cognitive Behavioural Therapy (if you're more convinced by science)

5 Happiness is all down to the way you think

It isn't situations and events that make you feel happy or unhappy – it's how you respond to them. Take Sonia and Hannah, for example. Sonia's a proper worry-wart, but Hannah's always bright and cheerful – sometimes they drive each other nuts!

These two can have exactly the same experience, such as watching the news on TV – and it can make Hannah feel glad and grateful, but Sonia anxious and unhappy. It's all down to the way they think.

Here's a table to show how thoughts can lead to happy or unhappy feelings.

Experience	Thought	Feeling
Neighbours *is* cancelled because of the cricket (why do they do that?)	*It's not fair – now my whole day is ruined!*	☹
	There might be something good on the other channels	☺
Spiteful Sara calls you a fat freak	*She's right – I look horrible*	☹
	She needs to get a life – I'm fine	☺
You get a new school bag, but not the £65 one you wanted	*I never get anything really cool*	☹
	Great – I've got a new school bag!	☺
Your teacher's starting a new drama club after school	*It'll probably be rubbish*	☹
	It's worth a try	☺
Your mates want to have a New Year party	*What's to celebrate? The end of one boring year and the start of another one*	☹
	I'll bring the crisps and cola!	☺

To find out if the way you think could be making you feel happy or unhappy, do the Attitude Test.

The Attitude Test

Think about each statement, then write down either agree or disagree.

1 *If I make a mistake I stop trying.* **agree/disagree**

2 *If I don't get my hopes up I won't be disappointed.* **agree/disagree**

3 *Nothing good ever happens to me.* **agree/disagree**

4 *I should be nicer/ cleverer/ better looking.* **agree/disagree**

5 *When I have a headache I worry that it might be caused by a brain tumour.* **agree/disagree**

6 *If someone's nasty to me I think no one likes me.* **agree/disagree**

7 *I lose sleep worrying about global warming/ crime/ terrorism.* **agree/disagree**

8 *I don't like trying new things in case I fail.* **agree/disagree**

9 *I've never done anything that I feel proud of.* **agree/disagree**

10 *Nothing I do makes any difference.* **agree/disagree**

All disagrees *Nice thinking – keep smiling!*
More than 7 disagrees *Not too bad.*
More than 7 agrees *Not too good.*
All agrees *Get down off that high bridge – all is not lost, because here's something a lot of people don't realize...*

Bonus fact

You can change the way you think!

I'm going to tell you how, but first I need to warn you about the high hill and the hobgoblin...

2

The high hill and the hobgoblin

If the people around you are negative thinkers, they might not like you suddenly becoming all upbeat, confident and optimistic. They might feel that you're leaving them behind. They might not understand it. They might even try to undermine you.

This is like when someone tries to give up smoking – all their friends who don't smoke are delighted and want to help, because they won't have to go on breathing in foul fumes. But all the ones who do smoke keep offering them cigarettes because they don't want to be the only ones stuck with a horrible habit.

And it isn't just other people who might find it hard. You might feel quite a lot of resistance inside yourself because there are actually a number of advantages to being down in the dumps.

Six reasons why it's good to be gloomy

1 You get sympathy

This is great, not just because people pay attention to you, but also because they'll often do things to try and cheer you up.

Have some of my chocolate

Do you want to come round to my house after school?

2 You aren't a threat to anyone

If you're happy and successful, some people might be jealous and try to spoil things for you. Staying gloomy means they don't have to bother.

17

3 You can get out of doing things

For example, your dad isn't going to make you take out the rubbish if you don't seem up to it – he's not a monster! And your mum won't make you do the washing up (though she might try to 'have a little talk' with you).

4 You can blame everybody else

If people don't manage to cheer you up – or maybe some heartless ones like your big bro don't even try to – then you can say it's their fault that you're unhappy. Blaming other people can be *sooo* satisfying.

5 It's not at all stressful

If you're too gloomy to do anything except sit around you don't have to set yourself goals and that means there's absolutely no risk of failure.

6 It's easy

When you're knocked down it's easier to stay down rather than pick yourself up again.

The high hill

Being happy sometimes takes a bit of effort, like climbing a high hill. Anyone can be happy when things are going great – it's when the smelly stuff hits the fan that you need happy attitudes to help you handle it (not literally!).

If you're naturally a bit downbeat and pessimistic it might be hard at first, like hill climbing is hard for people who aren't very fit. But the more you practise, the more you build up fitness and the easier it gets.

It might be tougher too if a lot of challenging things are going on in your life, in the same way that carrying a heavy rucksack makes hill-climbing harder.

But going up the happy hill means getting a brand new outlook, and anyone can do it if they want to.

The hobgoblin

Maybe you don't believe me. Maybe your dad's just forgotten he promised to take you to football or you've got a big zit on your chin or there weren't any chips left for tea, and you think 'Like it's possible to be happy now!'

That's the resistance setting in.

19

So think about your resistance and try to picture it. Imagine what it looks like. Is it droopy as a dishcloth, or bitter and twisted like your old Uncle George who never got the breaks? Or is it dark and fierce like a hobgoblin in a hole? *What is it saying?*

Draw a picture of it (don't worry if you're no Picasso). Describe it in words if you prefer (you don't have to be Shakespeare). This is just a bit of fun, and when it's done...

You can see what you're up against!

3

The brain invaders

Look at this diagram of a normal, happy brain.
You can see that it's stuffed full of positive attitudes.

The trouble is that if negative attitudes get in, they
can push the positive ones right out. There isn't room
in your brain for everything!

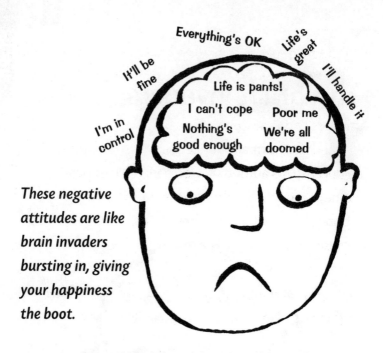

Everything's OK

Life's great

It'll be fine

I'll handle it

Life is pants!

I can't cope

Poor me

I'm in control

Nothing's good enough

We're all doomed

These negative attitudes are like brain invaders bursting in, giving your happiness the boot.

How do they get in?

Some people are naturally more prone to the glooms – it's in their genes, and almost everyone feels moody when their hormones kick in as they grow older.

Some people are overwhelmed by a difficult experience, such as an illness in the family or falling out with friends, and then they can slip into unhappy thinking.

Some people have to cope with horrible circumstances every day that make it very hard not to get depressed.

But lots of people who don't have any major problems go through life worrying and grumbling and feeling down because their heads are full of unhappy attitudes and they don't even realize it.

You don't normally notice the way you react to life because it's automatic. You absorb both positive and negative attitudes from your environment like a sponge on a wet surface, never questioning them because they just seem normal.

You can start noticing your automatic attitudes by thinking about your social environment

Family: do they grumble and stress a lot, or are they generally laid-back and positive?

Friends: do you all compete over who has the worst life, or are you just too busy enjoying yourselves?

Teachers: do they pile on the pressure or fill you with the fun of learning?

TV: do the programmes you watch make you feel that life's lovely or all gloom and doom?

Magazines and newspapers: do the ones you read make you feel good about yourself and your life?

Characters in books: actually, come to think of it, they usually have great attitudes because if they were just to give up and reach for the tissues there wouldn't be much of a story (so read lots of books!).

Catch-phrase clues

You can find clues about the attitudes you might have soaked up without noticing in the catchphrases people around you use. My grannie's was 'Mustn't grumble!' like I said, and my dad's was, 'Don't let it grind you down.' There are loads of little sayings and catchphrases, and everyone has their favourites...

Don't get your knickers in a knot

Onwards and upwards!

It's not fair!

Don't get your hopes up

I don't know why I bother

It's dog-eat-dog

Every cloud has a silver lining

It'll all end in tears

Catch a catch-phrase

Think about the little phrases your family and friends often come out with. You might not be able to think of many straight away, but start noticing them from now on. Notice your own catchphrases too.

What do your family and friends' catchphrases say about their attitudes to life?

How can you get the brain invaders out?

If your brain has been invaded by negative attitudes you can get rid of them by simply replacing them with positive ones, but of course you've got to notice them first.

So whenever you feel unhappy...

☁ *Check what thoughts are rattling around in your head*

☁ *Challenge those thoughts – are they true? Are they helpful?*

☁ *Choose a more cheerful way of looking at the situation*

My latest check-challenge-choose

The last time I was stuck in the glooms was when writing this book. I just couldn't get started. My daughter thought it was hilarious that my 'happy book' was making me so grumpy!

I checked what thoughts were rattling around in my head –

I challenged these thoughts. Were they helpful? Well, no! Were they true? I'd written lots of books like this one and I'd never missed a deadline in my life.

Plus, if a publisher wants to publish a book they must think that people will read it (and you're the living proof!).

Then I chose more positive attitudes which were both helpful and true –

As soon as I get stuck in, the work usually goes like a dream.

As soon as I finish it I'll think, 'That was fun!'

Then there will be interesting chats with my publisher sorting out the details...

...cover proofs so I can see how the book will look...

...letters and emails from my lovely readers...

I love this job!

So I told my daughter, 'You're right – it was funny me getting so grumpy about the happy book. But I can't sit around here chuckling all day – I've got writing to do!'

Now I want to tell you about Jordan. He made a mistake and then holed himself up in his bedroom, feeling horrible (what my old gran used to call 'going down the garden to eat worms').

He couldn't shake off his unhappy feelings so he did **check-challenge-choose**.

Jordan's check-challenge-choose

Jordan was watching *The Simpsons* when Loppy started whining to go out. It was a really funny bit, so Jordan ignored him. He forgot all about it until his mum got home and went ballistic at Loppy for doing a puddle by the back door.

Jordan felt really guilty. It would only have taken a few minutes to go and open the door. Now Loppy was in Mum's bad books and it was his fault. He didn't feel like watching TV any more. He didn't feel like doing anything.

After half an hour or so of lying on his bed feeling bad, Jordan stopped and noticed what thoughts were going round in his head.

Having checked his thoughts, he challenged them. Were they helpful? No, they made him feel miserable.

Were they true? Well, it was true that he should have let Loppy out, but he wasn't being deliberately selfish – he'd been meaning to do it as soon as the good bit was over, then just forgot. It was true he had got Loppy into trouble, but Loppy had the attention span of a peanut and he'd have forgotten about it as soon as Mum finished telling him off, if not before.

Jordan chose happier ways to think about the situation, which were all true too.

If Jordan had stayed 'down the garden eating worms' poor old Loppy would have been left watching TV on his own instead of leaping around the park.

Happy fact :-)

Sorting out your own negative thinking is great for the people around you too.

If I had stayed down in the dumps my publisher would still be waiting for the manuscript and my daughter would be tearing her hair out! This demonstrates another very interesting fact.

The more you do check-challenge-choose when you're down in the dumps, the less you have to. That's because, over time, positive attitudes can become automatic just like negative ones.

The check-challenge-choose clues
Certain words are a dead give-away that the brain invaders have got in. Whenever you feel fed up, check for the following.

 Nothing, never, nobody
(did you spot these in my ch-ch-ch?)

 Poor me!

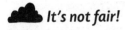 *It's not fair!*

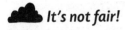 *Should, should, should*
   (did you spot these in Jordan's?)

 My life is pants!

If you find any of them lurking around in your thoughts, stop and challenge them right away. Give them the boot and fill up your brain with happy attitudes instead.

The brain invaders can be slippery customers so, to help you spot them, let's take a closer look at each one in turn...

It's not fair! Poor me! My life is pants!

Should, should, should

Nothing, never, nobody

31

4

Nothing, never, nobody

'**N**othing, never, nobody' are the tell-tale signs
for one of the commonest brain invaders – all-or-
nothing thinking.

This is when one little thing goes wrong and
you think, 'Nothing ever goes right for me.' When
something you wanted doesn't happen and you think,
'I never get what I want.' When you fall out with one
of your mates and you think, 'Nobody likes me.'

All-or-nothing thinking can also show up as
'Everything, always, everybody' too. 'Everything goes
wrong', 'I'm always left out', 'Everybody hates me.'

Check...
This kind of thinking is easy to spot by the tell-tale
words and it's also easy to challenge.

Challenge...
Is it helpful? Hmm... The words 'mountain' and
'molehill' spring to mind. Is it true? No. Real life

isn't all good or all bad – it's a mixture like a tube of Smarties with bright pinks and yellows alongside boring browns.

Choose...

When you feel a touch of the 'nothing-never-nobodys' coming on, choose to focus instead on the things that are going right for you, the ways that you are getting what you want and the people who aren't being horrible to you, and then you'll feel a whole lot more cheerful. That's what Karl did.

• • • • • • • **Karl's story** • • • • • • •

Karl's mum told him off for coming home late. Karl got into a major strop. 'She's always having a go at me,' he thought. He stomped off to his room and put on his music really loud to annoy her.

She went upstairs to tell him to turn it down. 'See?' thought Karl. 'She's doing it again!' He thought back over all the times she'd had a go at him before, like a prosecution lawyer building a case.

He could have carried on for hours. But Karl didn't want to have a miserable evening, so he stopped and

33

did check-challenge-choose. Was 'she's always having a go at me' a helpful way of thinking? Did it make him feel happy? No, it made him feel angry, and that made him act up.

Was it true? Karl stopped going over his grievances and tried to think of all the times his mum hadn't had a go at him when she could have. What about when his ball went through the greenhouse roof? And the day he accidentally left his little sister at the village shop?

His mum did have a go at him sometimes, but not all the time. On the whole, they got along pretty well. Maybe she'd only had a go this time because she felt worried about him. Actually, it was quite nice to know she cared!

● ● ● ● ● ● ● ● ● ● ● ● ●

The strange power of 'nothing, never, nobody'
All-or-nothing thinking works like a magnet, attracting negative experiences. For example, Karl thinking his mum was always having a go at him meant he felt like playing up and that meant she had a go again.

Supposing you think there's nothing to do in your neighbourhood, then you probably won't bother looking which means that you definitely won't find anything. If you think you're never going to get what you want, you're likely to stop trying – and then you definitely won't get it.

If you think 'Nobody likes me,' you'll probably be less friendly in case you're rejected – and then people won't have so much chance to like you.

Breaking the power

There's a magic word that can break the power of 'nothing, never, nobody' and that is **'some'**.

'Some things, sometimes, some people'

Did you notice that Karl used it? It worked for him and it will work for you.

Happy fact :-)

Getting rid of 'nothing, never, nobody' means not only that you feel better about your life – your life actually gets better too.

5

Poor me!

When you feel helpless or despondent, check for victim thinking. Tell-tale signs might include, 'I can't do anything about it' and 'It's not my fault' and 'Poor me!'

The appealing thing about victim thinking is that it means you don't have to make any effort – what's the point, since there's nothing you can do? The problem is that victim thinking stops you taking control and making things better for yourself.

You can challenge victim thinking with this simple and obvious fact:

Happy fact :-)

There is always something you can do.

Even when you can't control what happens to you, you can always choose how you want to react.

For example, Susie and her mum went on a camping weekend, but when they arrived they discovered that a mouse had got into the shed where the tent was stored and now the tent was full of holes. They had to pack up and go home.

Susie and her mum could have chosen to think 'Poor us! Our weekend is ruined.' They could have blamed the mouse or dad for leaving the shed door open or each other for not checking the tent was OK before they set off. They could have sat around moping until Sunday, but that would have been miserable.

Instead, they said, 'It's a pain but still, we've got the whole weekend free now so let's do some lovely day trips instead.' And they had a great time.

Victim thinking is quite hard to spot, so here's a quiz to help you find out if it's got into your brain.

Have you got victim thinking?

You are kept in at playtime because Ally and Jay wouldn't stop talking. Do you think:

1 That's my whole day down the toilet because of that selfish pair of idiots. Mrs P kept warning them but did they take any notice? Oh no! They don't care what happens to anyone else in the class, etc.

2 It's only one playtime, but it doesn't seem fair, so I'll complain to Mrs P if it happens again.

Your friend has a birthday party from 7–11pm and your dad says you're only allowed to stay till 10 o'clock. Do you think:

1 There's no point in going, it's so humiliating, my parents are such losers, etc.

2 I've only got three hours so I'd better make the best of it.

*You're on **The X Factor** and they don't put you through to the next round. Do you think:*

1 This was my dream and now they've ruined it.

2 I'm not good enough yet, but I've got a whole year to practise before next time.

Your friend was going to lend you a book but now he's given it to Marcus instead. Do you think:

1 I've been waiting ages for that book and I really wanted to read it and now I probably won't get a chance because Marcus isn't exactly an Olympic speed-reader, plus he's bound to give it to Alistair next...

2 I'd better get it out of the library.

Results

Mostly 1 *You've got a spot of victim thinking going on. Poor you!*

Mostly 2 *I like your can-do attitude – but I don't suppose you'd let it get you down if I didn't.*

Poor me – horrible you!

Did you notice in Susie's story and the quiz how feeling helpless can mean you start looking for someone else to blame? That's the other problem with victim thinking – it pitches you into pointless anger and is a pain for the people around you.

Here's Ms Moody, being a victim.

Now here she is **not** being a victim.

I'll phone for breakdown recovery. They won't take long.

Ms Moody has just demonstrated how not being a victim helps you:

1 Have better relationships

2 Find solutions

3 Feel happier

But...

Victim thinking can be very hard to get rid of because you always get resistance. When you ask yourself, 'Could I choose a better way of thinking about this?' up jumps the little hobgoblin yelling, 'Maybe I could, but why should I?'

It's always possible to blame someone else when things go wrong and maybe sometimes they really are to blame, so why should you let them off the hook? Well, it's not a question of letting them off the hook – it's a question of taking back your own power and feeling happy instead of helpless.

Supposing your dad's told you off for something you didn't do. That makes you feel fed up and it's his fault you're unhappy. Now you've got a choice – do you waste the rest of the day feeling angry and blaming him, hoping your bad mood will give him the message, or focus on what you can do to make yourself feel better?

Although it's easier to mope around blaming other people, you'll have much more fun if you let go of 'Poor me' and choose 'OK it's happened so what am I going to do about it?' instead.

6

It's not fair!

If you feel jealous or resentful, check for 'not fair' thinking. When you challenge 'not fair' thinking you can see that it isn't helpful – it doesn't make you feel happy. But it is true – life really isn't fair. Some people are naturally much better looking than others and some are much cleverer. And everybody's life is different – some people live in massive mansions and some people live in tiny terraces.

You can choose to deal with 'not-fair' thinking in four ways.

1 Accept that life really isn't fair – and be glad about it!

For life to be completely fair, we would all have to be exact clones of each other and live in identical houses, etc. That would be very boring, plus it would mean we'd have no one to look up to, and nothing to strive for.

> **Happy fact :-)**
>
> **Life isn't fair!**

2 Know you're not seeing the whole picture

There's a saying that you can't judge someone until you've walked a mile in their shoes and that's because you don't ever know the whole story. Are you jealous of a rich, famous pop star? Maybe you'd be less jealous if you knew that as well as being rich and famous she was also anorexic and miserable.

• • • • • • • Frankie's story • • • • • • •

Frankie was really jealous of his brother because he was a champion swimmer. Their dad spent every spare minute helping him with his training and he never had time for Frankie. It wasn't fair!

Frankie tried to keep his jealous feelings to himself, but one day they just spilled out. His brother was astonished. 'How do you think I feel?' he said. 'I have to get up at 6 o'clock every morning, while you're still in bed, drive across town with Dad, and spend an hour thrashing up and down an empty swimming pool. Then I have to do the same thing after school. I never get to go out with my mates or have a life, like you do. But I can't get out of it because it's so important to Dad. When I look at what you've got, it doesn't feel very fair to me.' After that, Frankie didn't feel so jealous because he wasn't just looking at one aspect of his brother's life (the attention he got from their dad), he was seeing a bit of the bigger picture.

● ● ● ● ● ● ● ● ● ● ● ●

3 Notice all the things you've got that other people haven't

Remember that 'not fair' works both ways – we're all richer, cleverer or better looking than someone, and even the things you might not like about your life, somebody else probably would.

4 Be grateful for what you have

The gratitude attitude

Even if you don't try anything else at all from this
book – try this. It's really good.

Think of five good things about today. They can
be good things about every day, such as trees or your
dad, or good things that happened specifically today,
like the pizza you had for lunch or the Jacqueline
Wilson book that's just got to the nail-biting bit.

*Count off the five things
on your fingers.*

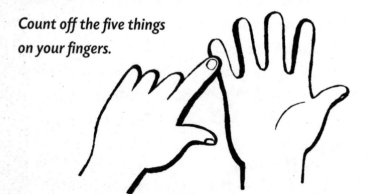

Now say thank you.

It's as easy as that, and if you do it every night before
you go to sleep, it will spread a little happiness into
every part of your life.

7

Should, should, should

Should is the kiss of death to happiness, so don't have any truck with it! (I've put three **shoulds** together because they multiply like rabbits if you're not careful – I **should**, you **should**, life **should**...).

Should takes you away from real life and into cloud cuckoo land, where everything's perfect and nothing ever goes wrong. It is the root of perfectionism, and perfectionism is a kind of madness.

Should makes you feel disappointed and resentful, because life can never measure up to your ideal of how it **should** be. Nothing is perfect – your friends, family, school... you yourself.

Find a piece of paper and complete the following
sentences to see where your **shoulds** are lurking:

My friends should...
For example, Tell me when they're going into town.

My family should...
For example, Have more days out together.

My teacher should...
For example, Stop giving us tests all the time.

I should...
For example, Be nicer to my brother.

Should isn't helpful and it isn't real. There are two
ways of getting rid of it.

1 Change the situation if you can

2 Accept the situation if you can't

Think about your answers above and see how you could get rid of your **shoulds**. In my example, you **could** ask your mates to tell you next time they're going into town, but if you've already done that and they ignored you, then you're just going to have to accept it and get over it – stop feeling hard done by and do something else instead. (Or get some new friends, of course.)

You **could** ask your mum and dad to have more days out as a family – maybe they didn't realize you'd like that. But if they can't – no time, no money – accept it and enjoy the bits of time you do have together.

You **could** tell your teacher you're fed up with tests. It's always worth saying what you want because otherwise how will anyone know? But if she says there's no choice, then you'll just have to accept it.

And you **could** think of ways to be nicer to your brother – keep working at it because you can't just get new brothers, but don't beat yourself up about it if you can't manage it all the time. You're only human!

Did you notice what happened to the **shoulds** as soon as we started looking at them in this way?

They turned into **coulds**! They stopped being a problem and became an opportunity. What a happy transformation!

> ## Happy fact :-)
> **Should is a problem that could be an opportunity.**

If you want to be happy, get rid of **should**. Accept that nobody's perfect, including you. Accept it and be grateful, because life's imperfections are what make life interesting. If everything was always lovely we'd die of boredom – imagine! It would be like a soap with no secrets and rows – *Eastenders* with everyone being nice to each other. Who'd want to watch that?

Could be better!

In an ideal world everything would be perfect, but in the real world everything is both good and bad – you help around the house, but you like to hog the bathroom – your rabbit looks sweet and cuddly, but he bites when you try to pick him up.

Changing your **shoulds** to **coulds** means that although you'll never make things perfect, you're trying to make them better. You **could** check no one's busting for a pee before you go for a soak in the bath, for example – that would be better. You **could** spend more time trying to bond with your rabbit.

Check-challenge-choosing when it comes to your **shoulds** won't bring you perfect happiness 24/7 (that's a myth like every other idea of perfection) but it will be a step on the way to helping yourself feel happier.

8

My life is pants!

If you feel just generally fed up with your life, check whether you're suffering from Junk Filter Brain. This is the equivalent of reading all your junk mail and deleting everything in your inbox. It's when you hold on to all the bad stuff and let the good stuff slip away without even noticing it.

JFB is a bit like the flu – some people get it worse than others and it can spread like wildfire. One person starts complaining about how hard they've got it, and soon it becomes a competition:

I hate my bedroom – it's too small...

At least you don't have to share it with your sister...

At least you've got a sister...

Junk Filter Brain is also known as glass-half-empty-syndrome, as in

When you find yourself thinking the glass is half empty, challenge that thought and you'll see that it is true. But it's also true that the glass is half full. So which way of looking at things is more helpful?

If you want to be happy, choose to focus on the good things in your life and let the bad ones go. Here are three techniques that might help you.

1 Look on the bright side

There are two sides to everything, so even when something bad happens, good things can come out of it. As Shakespeare said, 'Nothing is ever good or bad but thinking makes it so' (Shakespeare's always good for a quote!).

For example, what if you always have chicken korma when your family send out for takeaway because you love chicken korma, and then one night the restaurant's run out of chicken? That's a bad thing, right? You're going to have to pick something else. So you order beef biriani – and it turns out that beef biriani is humungously delicious, even better than chicken korma. Maybe the restaurant running out of chicken wasn't such a bad thing after all.

You don't always notice the bright side at all, but one way of making sure you do is by playing 'Bad news, good news.'

Bad news, good news

1 *Think of something you feel fed up about, for example, 'It's raining today.' That's the bad news.*

2 *Now think of something good about it, for example, 'We'll be allowed to stay in and play on the computers.'*

3 *Bad news? 'There aren't enough computers for everyone.'*

4 *Good news? 'We got one last time.'*

5 *Bad news? 'Miss might say we have to let someone else have a turn.'*

6 *Good news? 'We could play Date-marry-dump instead.'*

7 *Bad news? 'They might tease me about you-know-who.'*

8 *Good news...*

You get the picture!

The amazing thing is that this always works. Even something really bad, such as your local leisure centre burning down, can have good side effects, such as your whole community pulling together to rebuild it.

If you make a habit of looking on the bright side when you have small setbacks you'll know there always is one. That knowledge will help if you're ever in the middle of a major crisis and you just can't see how any good can come of it at all – you'll be able to trust that there is a silver lining and it will eventually be revealed.

Happy fact :-)

**Every cloud has
a silver lining.**

2 Focus on fun

Playing 'Bad news, good news' is a great way of seeing that even bad situations can have a good side. Making a happy scrapbook is a way of making sure you notice all the good ones.

Make a happy scrapbook!

You will need

■ One of those big scrapbooks you can buy in any stationer's shop, or a photo album or a loose leaf file

- Scissors
- Glue stick
- Pen

What to do

Every day, when something nice happens, get a memento. For example, if you go to tea at your gran's house, it might be the bus ticket or a copy of her world-beating biscuit recipe. It could be a blade of grass from the pitch you had football practice on, or a pic you took of your mates at the mall, or a cutting from a TV mag about a programme that made you laugh.

At the end of the day, cut and stick.

If you like writing, jot down something about what happened and why it made you feel happy ('Gran forgot she was making cheese scones and put cherries in as well. They weren't bad, considering...').

Every Sunday night, flick back over the week's happy scraps and just enjoy them.

3 Celebrate success

People say 'learn from your failures' – which is right – but they forget the other side of the coin, which is 'celebrate your successes'. An amazing number of people don't even notice their successes!

Success is an individual thing. If you're frightened of going on a bus on your own, then the first time you do it will be a major triumph, whereas for someone who does it every day it's no big deal. Lots of writers have a big launch party when their book is published, but I like to crack open the bubbly six months before that when I deliver the manuscript, because I've finished the writing and that's the hardest part for me.

You can celebrate any time – you don't have to wait till you win the Nobel Peace Prize or get voted Junior Citizen of the Century. In fact, why not have a celebration right now?

Have a celebration!

First...
get some nice nibbles and a bottle of something fizzy
Then...
invite some mates over**
Then...
everyone thinks of something to celebrate****
Finally...
enjoy yourselves!

* Or do it on your own if you're not very sociable
** Or just you if you haven't invited anyone round

Do I hear you say, 'But what if I haven't got anything to celebrate?' You've **always** got something to celebrate!

For example, in the last few weeks you might have:

Got up in time for breakfast every day.

Plucked up the courage to try the local youth club.

Remembered someone's birthday.

Got a better grade than usual.

☁ *Saved some pocket money.*

☁ *Bought something bold and beautiful to wear.*

☁ *Learnt to bake a cake (a useful skill when it comes to celebrating).*

☁ *Not lost your temper with your little bro.*

☁ *Written something for the school newsletter.*

☁ *Done any other thing that might be hard or unusual for you.*

Before you read on, stop and think about your recent successes. Write them down. Don't worry how small they might seem to someone else. Call this your 'I did it' list and add things as they occur to you.

Celebrating your personal successes doesn't just mean you'll notice the good stuff and have a great time – it also means you'll become more aware of the good possibilities that are open to you. So you baked your first cake – could you try making biscuits next? So you wrote something for the school newsletter – could you enter a writing competition? (If the answer's yes, celebrate entering – you don't have to wait to see if you've won.)

Filter, decide, delete!

Life sends you nasty stuff sometimes – stuff you don't want, such as arguments with your friends, bad-tempered parents, boring lessons, spiders under your bed.

But most of the time it bombards you with brilliant stuff such as clouds and sunshine and larking around, friends, soccer, gossip, music, badgers, TV, your mum's smile, your teacher's jokes...

With Junk Filter Brain, you hold on to the rubbish and delete your inbox. If you want to be happy the trick is to ignore the junk and just pick up the good stuff instead.

9

Your positive past

There's nothing like happy memories for making you feel good, but sometimes looking back can have the opposite effect. If you find yourself obsessing over the past and getting stuck in a cycle of yearning or regret, check for the brain invaders, because they can get into your memories just as they can get into your everyday thoughts.

Nothing, never, nobody

If these three get in they are a recipe for self-pity, as in, 'Nothing ever went right for me', 'I never got what I wanted' and 'Nobody ever cared' (boo, hoo!).

A quick challenge will certainly reveal that some things did go right, sometimes you did get what you wanted and there was always someone who cared (even if it was just your hamster).

Poor me!

Victim attitudes can show up in your thoughts about the past as 'There was nothing I could do.'

If you challenge this you'll notice that there was something you could do, because you did it. Maybe you couldn't prevent something happening, but you certainly did choose how to react to it.

Supposing someone was nasty to you at school – you could have told a teacher, you could have got into a fight, you could have talked it over with your friends – even if you didn't do anything at all, that was still your choice. Get rid of 'Poor me' in the past by taking responsibility for your actions – maybe you didn't always make good choices, but if you know that, you'll make better ones next time.

Not fair!

What can I say? It isn't fair now and it wasn't fair then. Just remember the antidote – the gratitude attitude. Do it now – five great things you had when you were younger.

The first five that came into my head were: making mud pies on the back step, my mum's chocolate cake, The Famous Five, holidays on Hayling Island, my red school shoes. My list shows that the great things don't have to cost a lot of money – they're great because they gave you so much pleasure, and they're unique to you.

Should, should, should

'I should have won that competition', 'Dad shouldn't have told me off', 'We should have bought that big house on Parkside.' Time for a reality check – it wasn't an ideal world in the past any more than it is now. 'Should' is a recipe for anger and resentment in the past just as it is in the present.

It's also a recipe for regret, 'I shouldn't have said that mean thing', 'I should have worked harder for my exam', 'I should have helped more when Mum was ill.'

If you don't want to get stuck in the past, it's important to know how to deal with regrets, and it's really very simple. When you've done something you think you shouldn't have done...

1 *Say sorry*
2 *Make amends*
3 *Learn from your mistakes*
4 *Forgive yourself and let go*

• • • • • • • Jesse's story • • • • • • •

Jesse lost her temper with the computer, smashed the mouse down on the table and stormed off to watch TV. No one saw what happened, and no one noticed that the mouse was broken until after tea, when Jesse's dad wanted to go online. He was so cross to find the mouse was smashed that Jesse panicked and said her little brother had done it. Her little brother had to go straight to bed.

Jesse felt bad about it. 'I shouldn't have done that,' she thought. The next day, she said sorry to her little brother and offered to do his chores for him. She said sorry to her Dad, and offered to buy a new mouse.

She knew she would never tell lies and get her brother into trouble again. It had been a mistake, and everybody makes mistakes. So she forgave herself and stopped feeling miserable about it.

• •

Even if you did something way back in the past that you shouldn't have done, you could still do something about it. You could still say sorry, if you haven't already, and you could still try to make amends.

Then you could let yourself off the hook, because you've done all you can. (Did you notice how changing 'should' to 'could' works in the past as well as in the present?)

My life has been pants!

This brings me to a very interesting thing – the past isn't real. The facts are, of course – such as the fact that yesterday was Thursday and that I was born in Hampshire – but memories are stories you build up around the facts, and you can choose what kind of stories they are.

Let me demonstrate. Recently I went to a weekend conference in Oxford with 350 other children's writers and illustrators. Those are the facts. Here are two different stories about it, both of which are true.

☁ My rotten weekend

There were roadworks for miles on the M4 and then I took a wrong turning, so I finally arrived at the conference late and tired.

I met so many people that I couldn't remember their names, and the noise in the dining hall and corridors really got to me. I wanted to hook up with old friends, but it was hard to find them in the crowd. I didn't learn much in the talks and sessions.

I left early on the Sunday because I'd had enough.

 My brilliant weekend

There were roadworks on the M4 so I had plenty of time in the car to think about the next chapter of my book, and I had some nice ideas.

There was a great buzz in the dining hall and corridors, with lots of new people to meet and I kept bumping into old friends. The talks didn't tell me anything I didn't already know, but that meant I could sit back and listen without feeling I had to take notes.

I left early on Sunday because I wanted to have tea with my son before heading home.

You can choose to have happy memories by focusing on the good stuff and letting the bad stuff go. (Or you can play up the bad stuff and make a joke of it, if you're a comedian.)

All your memories are stories, and you pick and choose from them to create your life story. Some people build a tragic story by choosing to remember painful things, and some people build a happy story by choosing cheerful memories.

Your happy life story

1 Get the facts

Take your time. You need the facts to hang the story on. If you don't know, ask your mum and dad. Jot things down under these three headings.

Your first year

You might be surprised to find big gaps in what you know about yourself. For example, where were you born? In hospital? Which hospital? What time of day was it? What was the weather like? What were your parents' jobs at the time? How old were your brothers and sisters, if you had any? What was the name of the house or road you lived in? Did you go to a nursery? Or a child minder?

Pre school

Did you go to a playgroup or nursery school? Who were your friends? What was your favourite toy?

School

How many schools have you been to? What were they called? Where were they and how did you get to them? Who were your teachers? What were your favourite lessons?

2 Choose some happy experiences

The facts are neutral – not happy or unhappy.
To build them into a happy story, you need to select experiences that made you feel happy, so for each period think of the following.

one thing you liked doing

one thing you felt proud of

one event you really enjoyed

one person you really loved

3 Choose more happy experiences

In fact, keep going until you get fed up with it.

4 Keep choosing happy!

You don't have to write down your whole life story – unless you want to. It's a very interesting thing to do because nothing's more fascinating than you yourself. (If you're not very confident about your writing skills, get my book *How to be a Brilliant Writer* – it'll really help you!) It's enough to understand how memory works, that it's all stories, and how unhappy or happy you think your life has been depends largely on which stories you choose to focus on when you look back and how you choose to tell them.

So there you have it. If you want to be happy, remember the good stuff and let go of the bad.

10

Your fabulous future

Are you an optimist or a pessimist? When you think about the future, do you expect the best or the worst to happen? This quick quiz will help you to find out. (If you're thinking, 'What's the point, it probably won't tell me anything' you can assume you're a pessimist and skip to the next bit!)

Are you an optimist or a pessimist?

1 *They're doing auditions for the school play and you really want to be in it. Do you:*

A Practise hard, go along and give it your best shot.

B Go but don't practise beforehand because you might be wasting your time.

C Not go because they probably won't choose you anyway.

2 *It's your birthday and you want to have a barbecue on the beach. Do you:*

A Send out the invitations and buy the sausages and marshmallows.

B Send out the invitations but leave the shopping till the last minute – if it rains, you might have to cancel.

C Decide to go to the cinema instead – it's not so good, but it won't matter if it rains.

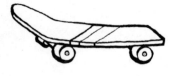

3 *Your mates are starting a petition to get the council to build a skateboard ramp. Do you:*

A Sign up and take extra forms so your neighbours and family can sign too.

B Sign up because you might as well.

C Not bother because no one's going to take any notice of what kids want, right?

4 *You're coming up to end of year tests. Do you think:*

A The questions might be easy.

B The questions might be hard.

C The questions will be impossible so I'm staying home with a headache.

Results

Mostly A *You're an optimist, and everything's probably going to work out fine (but you already know that!).*
Mostly B *You aren't quite an optimist and you aren't quite a pessimist – sitting on the fence might get a bit uncomfortable (but then again, it might not!).*
Mostly C *You're a pessimist – no good will come of it!*

If you read back over the quiz you'll notice that expecting the best has an unexpected bonus – it means you are able to put all your energy into achieving your goals – and that gives you the best possible chance of succeeding. Expecting the worst means you're less likely to be successful because you probably won't even try. Psychologists call this 'self-sabotage' – it means you know what you want but you stop yourself getting it by harbouring unhelpful attitudes.

Pessimism doesn't only stop you trying hard and succeeding – it stops you feeling happy too. Instead of living your life in anticipation of good things, it makes you feel anxious and despondent.

Suppose a theatre group is visiting your school
in two weeks' time – if it turns out that they're
terrible, optimists will have had two weeks of
happy anticipation before the disappointment,
and pessimists will have had two weeks of gloomy
anticipation, but they'll still be disappointed too.

Where does pessimism come from and how can you get rid of it?

Pessimism is one of those attitudes that seep in from
your environment without you even noticing. If your
friends and family say, 'You shouldn't get your hopes
up' because, 'You might be disappointed,' and if they
think it's not worth trying because you'll probably fail,
or that things generally go from bad to worse – then
you might assume that this is a sensible, realistic way
of looking at things.

It's another case for
check, challenge, choose!

Check
Do you often expect that things will get worse or go wrong?

Challenge
Is that a helpful attitude? Well, let me see...
It stops you trying and makes you feel fed up.
Hmm... Is it true? No! The fact is no one knows
what will happen in the future. It's no more sensible
to assume that things will get worse than to assume
that they'll get better.

Choose
As either way is equally right or wrong, you might
as well choose to believe that everything will turn
out fine. That way, you can move forward feeling
much more confident and hopeful.

The return of the hobgoblin!

If the people around you are pessimistic thinkers
they might find your new optimistic attitude:
1 irritating
2 alarming
3 foolish

They might try to change your mind.

You might feel the same kind of resistance in yourself. Expecting the worst can feel safer because you imagine it'll mean you'll be ready if things go wrong, so switching to expecting the best can feel a bit alarming.

But as no one knows what life has in store for them you can't ever really be ready. You have to trust that whatever happens, you'll handle it. And you will. Look back for a minute – has anything bad ever happened to you? Of course it has. Did you survive? Even when something awful happens, like your dog dies, and you feel your heart is breaking inside your body, you somehow find a way to handle it because you have to.

In fact, setbacks make you stronger. If you expect the best, and maybe you're disappointed, well that's when you find out that you can get over it.

Happy fact :-)

Whatever happens,
you'll handle it.

Catastrophic thinking

This is kind of advanced pessimism. It's when you feel really worried that something completely catastrophic is going to happen, and it's incredibly common. Where does it come from? Mostly TV.

Look at these three lists and write down anything you've felt worried about in the last few months.

Catastrophe check lists

List 1

being blown up by terrorists

being caught in a flood

being a victim of crime

ecological disaster caused by global warming

catching bird flu, MRSA or any other dangerous infection

List 2

☁ being abducted by aliens

☁ meeting a sinister stranger

☁ going into hospital with an ingrown toe nail
   and ending up on life support

☁ having a sudden spate of poisonings in your
   street that no one seems to be investigating
   except a bad-tempered detective and his sergeant

☁ discovering ghosts in your garden

List 3

☁ finding out that the person you thought was your
   mum is actually your auntie, who bashed your
   real mum over the head with an ashtray just after
   you were born and buried her under the patio

☁ being caught in a fire started by a shady local
   businessman trying to fiddle his insurance

being the only tissue match for your worst enemy who used to be your best friend and suddenly needs a new kidney

falling foul of your unfriendly neighbourhood drug-dealing gang for something you didn't do

having a crush on someone who turns out to be a long-lost sister you never even knew you had

If you wrote down some from List 1 you're probably watching too many news programmes
If you wrote down some from List 2 you're probably watching too many dramas and serials
If you wrote down some from List 3 you're definitely watching too many soaps!

(If you wrote down some from each of the three lists, it might be a good idea to switch off and get a life!)

You can do check-challenge-choose with catastrophic thinking as you can with pessimism.

Is it helpful? **Duh!**

Is it true? No. Statistically, the chance of any of the dire things in these three lists happening to you is absolutely tiny.

So choose a better and more realistic way of thinking. Bad things happen to some people, but it's a lot more likely that nothing much will happen to you at all!

Your forward focus

When you think about the future, think positive. Get rid of pessimistic thoughts by always expecting the best. Stop catastrophic thinking by getting real. People say: 'Cheer up, it might never happen.' I say: 'Cheer up, because it almost certainly won't.'

11

Boosting your happy activities

Just as certain attitudes can make you feel happy or unhappy, so can certain activities. One way of becoming happier is by boosting your happy activities.

Research shows that the activity that makes people feel happiest is Scottish country dancing (yes, this is completely true!). What makes Scottish country dancing so great is:

1 The exercise

It's been scientifically proven that doing exercise of any kind boosts the level of serotonin (happiness chemicals) in the brain. A short walk every day can have the same effect on your mood as taking an antidepressant pill.

2 The lively music

Upbeat music makes you feel upbeat – it's as simple as that.

Happy fact :-)

Natural daylight also boosts your serotonin level, so dancing out of doors would be the bee's knees of happy activities.

3 Mixing with other people

This is great for your confidence if you're a bit shy, and sharing a sport or hobby can be a starting point for interesting new relationships, as well as strengthening existing ones.

Note

Though most people like joining in, some people are naturally happier doing their own thing. If you've had enough of being sociable after a whole day at school, don't force yourself to join a club in the pursuit of happiness – that would just be silly!

4 Developing new skills

Learning new things is an adventure and being good at something makes you feel good about yourself, no matter what it is.

5 Having a laugh

If you've ever tried Scottish country dancing, you'll know what I mean. When everyone goes galloping round to the left at top speed there's a fifty-fifty chance that you'll go galloping off to the right.

Laughter is a top tonic, scientifically proven to make people feel better in every way, including physically. Laughing helps you stay more healthy and recover more quickly when you are ill.

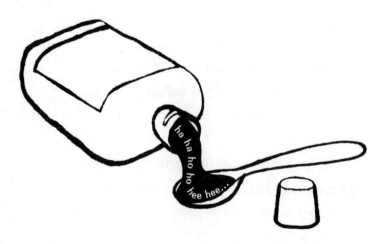

> ## Happy fact :-)
> A laugh a day keeps
> the doctor away.

If by any chance you don't fancy putting on a kilt and leaping around, you can still get the main benefits of Scottish country dancing doing other things.

For example:

- *sports give you physical exercise and social contact, and sometimes a bit of a laugh (depending on how bad you are)*

- *watching something funny on TV with your family gives you social contact and laughter*

- *having a make-over day with your mates is sociable, funny and skill-building, plus you're going to be listening to great sounds*

Besides having all the happy ingredients of social contact, music, exercise, skills and laughter, there's one more thing that's brilliant about Scottish country dancing – it's absolutely pointless. Scottish country dancing isn't going to make you rich or help you to understand fractions and that's great because happy activities are mostly things that you do just for fun.

Happy one-offs

As well as sports and hobbies that are part of your lifestyle, you can have happy one-offs, too. Try to do one completely pointless thing every day. Make three 'Just because I want to' lists right now, to help you get started.

Three 'Just because I want to' lists

'Just because I want to' ideas come in three categories.

1 Things you could do today

For example, paint your toenails green (you might have to go to the shops first), find out what a pomegranate tastes like (ditto), make a 'Have a nice day' card for your mum, try a new soap, ask all your mates to tell you a joke, step on the cracks and see if the bears get you...

2 Things you could set up today to do another day

For example, play five-a-side against the dads, have a day at the seaside, visit a museum, have a DVD-and-popcorn party.

3 Things you could never ever do even if they're tempting

For example, put a spider down Becca's back (haven't you heard of animal rights?), tell your teacher she looks a nightmare in that orange and turquoise top, eat everything in the fridge, set off the fire alarm, spray paint rude words on the pavement... I'd better stop here in case I give you ideas. This list is your 'just-because-I-want-to' sin bin – it's where all the things you think of when you're getting ideas for the first two categories have to go if they're unkind, stupid or illegal. Sorry!

Work your way through lists 1 and 2.
When you've done one, cross it off.
When you run out, write some more.

Helping other people

Doing a good deed every day is a better happiness boost than having more money – that's a scientific fact! You don't have to give up all your free time to feel the benefits. Your good deed can be something as small as making your mum a cup of tea or holding the door open for your teacher.

Or you can think a bit bigger and maybe offer to take out the rubbish or weed the flowerbeds or do some vacuuming.

Or you can think longer term, and offer to serve on the school council or join a community project.

Everything you do that makes someone else feel happy reflects back on you, and makes you feel happy too. If you don't believe me, try it and see.

Busy doing nothing

The joy of doing absolutely nothing has been almost lost in our modern culture of busyness and targets, and lots of people feel guilty about wasting time. We talk about 'spending time' as if we're at the shops, and we need something in return. In other parts of the world people would find that attitude very peculiar.

The problem with always rushing around and filling every second with TV or music or games, is that we don't notice the detail of what's going on around us, and so we miss out on lots of amazing stuff that can make us feel 'surprised by joy' (that's a quote from William Wordsworth – a great poet from the old days).

Einstein, who was a clever person I'm sure you'll agree, said you can live life in either of two ways –

as if everything is a miracle ... or nothing is.

When you take time out to look around, and notice the detail, that's when the miracle feeling can come in.

The miracle moment

At least once every day, stop.

Stop right where you are.

Look around.

What can you see?

A leaf, maybe, or a fly on a chip paper. A skateboard,
a cat on a wall, a cloud, a pavement, a shiny car.
An orange curtain, an iPod, a double-choc cookie,
your own hand.

Choose one thing to look at, anything at all, and
really look. Notice its colours and textures. Listen to
its sounds, if it has any. Isn't it incredible?

Do this right now. Every single thing is a miracle,
and we're too busy being busy even to notice it.

So there you have it. For maximum happiness,
take up a hobby that means all or any of these:

mixing with other people
  getting physical
    hearing great music
      learning new skills
        having a laugh

Treat yourself to happy one-offs just because you want to, help other people and take a few minutes every day to do ...

absolutely nothing at all.

12

The happy recap

You may not remember this now (your brain isn't big enough to hold everything!) but the very first fact I put in this book was 'Even happy people can't be happy all the time.' Life isn't perfect, which means that sometimes things go wrong and you are bound to feel unhappy.

Happy fact :-)

Trying to be happy all the time is unrealistic – it will end in tears!

Happy people accept that sometimes they will have problems and setbacks – they're just really good at bouncing back.

Negative attitudes weigh you down like a diet of cheesy chips and it's really hard to bounce with a head full of 'nothing, never, nobody', 'poor me', 'not fair', 'should' and 'pants!' It's also hard to move forward if you're full of fear and pessimism or you don't have many positive activities to energize you.

The way you think and behave can make you feel unhappy, but you don't have to let it.

It's as easy as ABC

So here it is in a nutshell – how to be happy.

A *Decide that you want to be happy and believe it will happen (optimism – nice!)*

B *When you're down in the dumps, check-challenge-choose your thinking*

C *Boost your happy activities*

The happy habit

Happy people are good news for everybody else – they don't feel the need to make other people feel miserable, or damage property, or sit around grumbling and complaining. They also tend to be more healthy, motivated and successful than unhappy people.

It's easy to develop positive attitudes when things are mostly going well, so start practising!

It's also easy to boost up your happy activities when you're feeling generally OK, so start that right now too.

Happy attitudes and activities can soon become a habit and having the happy habit will help you to enjoy life even more when things are going well and cope with it even better when they aren't.

Onwards and upwards!

This is my personal all-time favourite catch phrase and it's also the perfect note to end this book on, because being happy is like walking up a high hill – hard work sometimes but fantabuloso when you get to the top.

Note

Hooray – now I've finished the writing. This calls for a celebration! By a spooky coincidence, you've finished the reading now too, so I guess it could be celebration time for you!

More serious note

Although happy attitudes and activities are always helpful when it comes to coping with difficult circumstances, sometimes things happen to you which are so overwhelming that it simply isn't possible to bounce back.

If this happens to you don't feel bad about it – it can happen to anyone. But don't stay stuck – get help. Talk to your mum or dad, gran or grandpa, teacher, school counsellor or friend, or check out the helplines over the page, because a problem shared really is a problem halved.

ChildLine

Telephone: *0800 1111 – lines are open 24 hours a day*

Text: *0800 400 222 – weekdays 9.30am–9.30pm, weekends 9.30am–8pm*

Calls to ChildLine are free and don't show up on itemised phone bills from landlines, 3, BT Mobile, Fresh, Orange, TMobile, Virgin and Vodafone.

Samaritans

Telephone: *08457 909090*

email: *jo@samaritans.org*

Calls to Samaritans are charged at local rates.